DL

KEY FIGURES OF WORLD WAR II

BIOGRAPHIES OF WAR

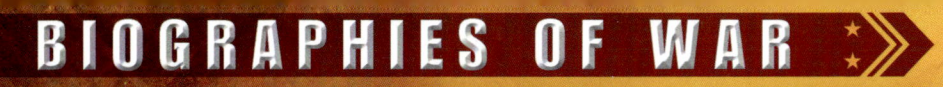

KEY FIGURES OF WORLD WAR II

EDITED BY
CATHERINE ELLIS

Britannica
Educational Publishing
IN ASSOCIATION WITH
ROSEN
EDUCATIONAL SERVICES

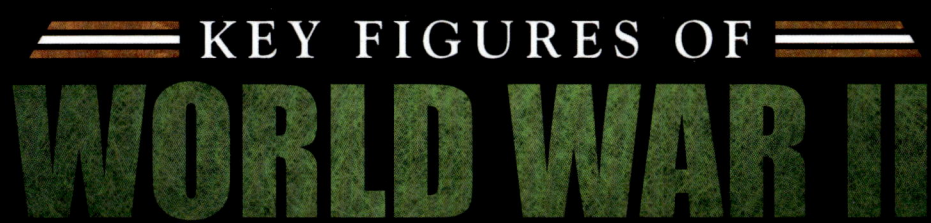

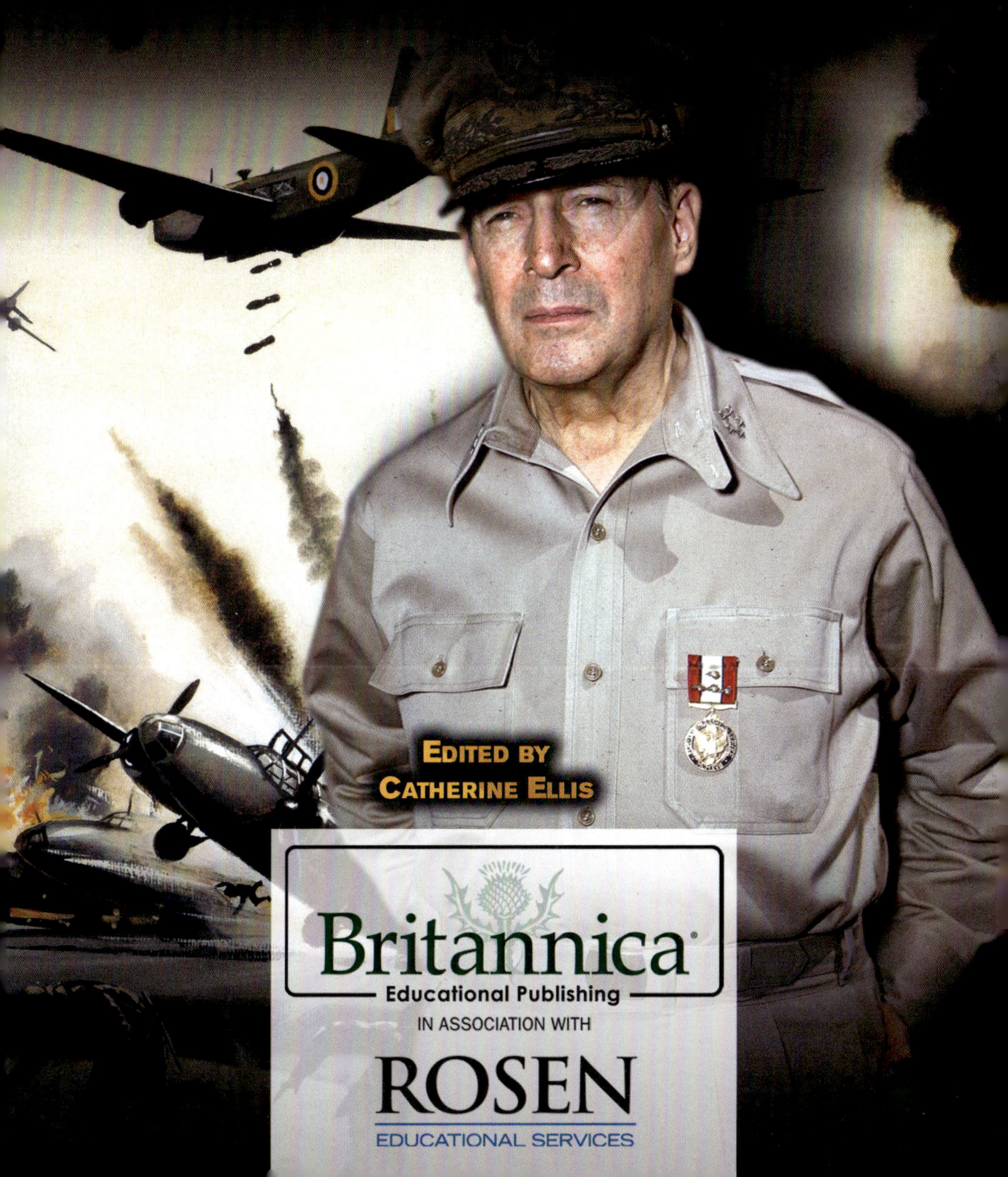

Published in 2016 by Britannica Educational Publishing (a trademark of Encyclopædia Britannica, Inc.) in association with The Rosen Publishing Group, Inc.
29 East 21st Street, New York, NY 10010

Copyright © 2016 by Encyclopædia Britannica, Inc. Britannica, Encyclopædia Britannica, and the Thistle logo are registered trademarks of Encyclopædia Britannica, Inc. All rights reserved.

Rosen Publishing materials copyright © 2016 The Rosen Publishing Group, Inc. All rights reserved.

Distributed exclusively by Rosen Publishing.
To see additional Britannica Educational Publishing titles, go to rosenpublishing.com.

First Edition

Britannica Educational Publishing
J.E. Luebering: Director, Core Reference Group
Anthony L. Green: Editor, Compton's by Britannica

Rosen Publishing
Hope Lourie Killcoyne: Executive Editor
Amelie von Zumbusch: Editor
Nelson Sá: Art Director
Michael Moy: Designer
Cindy Reiman: Photography Manager

Library of Congress Cataloging-in-Publication Data

Key figures of World War II/edited by Catherine Ellis.—First edition.
    pages cm.—(Biographies of war)
Includes bibliographical references and index.
ISBN 978-1-68048-057-3 (library bound)
1. World War, 1939–1945—Biography—Juvenile literature. 2. Generals—Biography—Juvenile literature. 3. Heads of state—Biography—Juvenile literature. I. Ellis, Catherine. II. Title: Key figures of World War Two.
D736.K435 2016
940.53092'2—dc23

2014039056

Manufactured in the United States of America

Photo credits: Cover and p. 3 (MacArthur), pp. 50, 70 Hulton Archive/Getty Images; cover and p. 3 (background) The National Archives/SSPL/Getty Images; pp. 6–7 ITAR-TASS/Sovfoto; pp. 6–7 (background) Paul Whitfield/Dorling Kindersly/Getty Images; p. 13 © Photos.com/Thinkstock; pp. 15, 42–43, 73, 75 Encyclopædia Britannica, Inc.; pp. 16–17 New Times Paris Bureau Collection/USIA/NARA; pp. 20–21, 90 Hugo Jaeger/The Life Picture Collection/Getty Images; pp. 22–23 Topical Press Agency/Hulton Archive/Getty Images; pp. 26–27 National Archives, Washington, D.C.; pp. 30–31 From J.P. Mallmann Showell, U-Boats under the Swastika (1987); pp. 32–33 Paul Popper/Popperfoto/Getty Images; p. 35 UPI/Bettmann Archive; pp. 38–39 U.S. Air Force; pp. 46–47 Mondadori/Getty Images; pp. 52–53, 56 Library of Congress Prints and Photographs Division; p. 59 U.S. Navy Photo; p. 61 U.S. Army Photo; p. 63 SSPL/Getty Images; p. 67 Keystone-France/Gamma-Keystone/Getty Images; p. 77 Universal Images Group/Getty Images; p. 79 Tass/Sovfoto; p. 83 H. Roger-Viollet; p. 85 The Life Images Collection/Getty Images; pp. 87, 97 AFP/Getty Images; p. 94 Heinrich Hoffmann, Munich; interior pages background textures Eky Studio/Shutterstock.com, Sfio Cracho/Shutterstock.com, Attitude/Shutterstock.com, macknimal/Shutterstock.com, Valentin Agapov/Shutterstock.com; back cover Oleg Zabielin/Shutterstock.com.

CONTENTS

J
940.53092
ELL

INTRODUCTION 6

CHAPTER ONE
EARLY STAGES OF THE WAR   **9**

CHAPTER TWO
A HARD-WON VICTORY   **29**

CHAPTER THREE
AMERICAN LEADERS   **49**

CHAPTER FOUR
OTHER ALLIED LEADERS   **66**

CHAPTER FIVE
AXIS LEADERS   **82**

CONCLUSION 99
GLOSSARY 100
FOR MORE INFORMATION 103
BIBLIOGRAPHY 107
INDEX 108

INTRODUCTION

Some 20 years after the end of World War I, lingering disputes erupted in an even larger and bloodier conflict—World War II. The war began in Europe in 1939, but by its end in 1945 it had involved nearly every part of the world. The opposing sides were the Axis Powers—consisting mainly of Germany, Italy, and Japan—and the Allies—primarily France, Great Britain, the United States, the Soviet Union, and, to a lesser extent, China. Estimates of the number of casualties vary widely, but by any measure the war's human cost was enormous—35 million to 60 million deaths, with millions more wounded or left homeless.

British Prime Minister Winston Churchill, U.S. President Franklin Roosevelt, and Soviet Premier Joseph Stalin meet at the Yalta Conference in February 1945 to discuss the final stages of the war.

KEY FIGURES OF WORLD WAR II

The political consequences of World War II, like those of World War I, altered the course of 20th-century world history. The war resulted in the Soviet Union's dominance of the countries of eastern Europe and eventually enabled a communist movement to take power in China. It also marked a decisive shift of power away from the countries of western Europe and toward the United States and the Soviet Union. The tense rivalry between those two countries and their allies, known as the Cold War, would influence events throughout the world for the next 50 years.

As is the case with all wars, the political and military leaders of the countries involved helped determine the outcome of World War II. The first chapters of this book offer a year-by-year account of the major events in the war, while the following ones contain profiles of some of the most important figures from both sides of the war. However, it is worth remembering that the war's outcome also depended on the action of many less well-known leaders, as well as countless soldiers, politicians, and citizens.

CHAPTER ONE

EARLY STAGES OF THE WAR

The outbreak of World War II followed a series of warlike acts between 1931 and 1939 by Japan, Italy, and Germany. The League of Nations proved ineffective in halting the aggression of Japan in China, the Italian invasion of Ethiopia, and the German takeover of Austria.

Britain and France agreed to let the German dictator Adolf Hitler and the Italian dictator Benito Mussolini take the territories they wanted. The British and French hoped this policy of appeasement would prevent another war.

On September 30, 1938, Britain and France agreed in Munich to let Germany have a part of Czechoslovakia called the Sudetenland. Hitler said this would be his last territorial demand in Europe. In March 1939 Hitler broke this pact, taking over the rest of Czechoslovakia. This ended the British and French policy of appeasement.

Prime Minister Neville Chamberlain of Great Britain and Premier Édouard Daladier of France promised aid to Poland in case of a Nazi attack. Hitler soon demanded the return of Danzig (Gdańsk) to Germany and a strip of territory linking East Prussia with the rest of Germany. Poland refused.

In May 1939 Germany and Italy signed a pact pledging to support each other in war. Hitler and other German leaders believed Germany lost World War I because it had to fight on two fronts. To prevent this in a new war Hitler and the Soviet dictator Joseph Stalin signed a ten-year nonaggression pact on August 23, 1939. On September 1 Germany annexed Danzig and invaded Poland, and the war began.

THE WAR DURING 1939

On September 3, 1939, two days after the invasion of Poland, Britain and France demanded that Germany withdraw its troops. When Germany refused, Britain and France declared war on Germany.

THE CONQUEST OF POLAND AND THE "PHONY WAR"

The Poles were easily defeated by Germany's blitzkrieg, or "lightning war." The first day the German Luftwaffe (air force) destroyed Poland's airfields and bases. Within a week it had crippled the lines of communication. At the same time German panzer (armored and mechanized) divisions encircled the Polish armies.

The Soviet Union invaded eastern Poland on September 17. Poland was soon forced to surrender. Germany and the Soviet Union divided Poland between them.

Some Polish government officials, soldiers, pilots, and naval units managed to escape the swift Nazi and Soviet advances. They fled to Britain, where they continued the fight against Germany with the Allies.

After Poland's defeat, the Western Front saw little fighting for about six months. This period is known as the "phony war." The war at sea, however, was active. Germany launched a counter-blockade against the British. German submarines (U-boats), mines, and bombs sank many Allied merchant and passenger ships.

SOVIET-FINNISH WAR

The Soviet Union invaded Finland on November 30. Finland had refused to give the Soviets military bases. The large Soviet army was expected to defeat tiny Finland quickly. The Finns, however, held off the Soviets for several months.

Finland's Mannerheim Line of fortifications was finally broken through early in 1940. On March 12 Finland signed a peace treaty that gave the Soviet Union important Finnish territory.

THE WAR DURING 1940

Early in April Germany invaded Denmark and Norway. Denmark accepted the "protection" that Germany offered the two countries. Norway, however, declared war.

British troops landed in Norway, but they were unable to stop the German advance. In May the British forces were evacuated. On June 9 Norway fell.

INVASION OF THE LOW COUNTRIES

On May 10 German forces invaded Belgium, the Netherlands, and Luxembourg. Luxembourg was occupied without resistance. Belgium and the Netherlands declared war.

In Britain, Chamberlain resigned and Winston Churchill replaced him as prime minister. The Allies sent troops into the Low Countries, but by May 14 the Dutch army had to give up the fight. The Netherlands was quickly brought under the rule of German occupation forces.

On May 13 German armored forces broke through Allied lines in the lightly defended Ardennes Forest of southern Belgium. Their columns drove through to the English Channel, cutting off British and French troops in northern France and Belgium. King Leopold of Belgium surrendered his army on May 28. The Allies had no choice but to escape by sea, evacuating 360,000 soldiers from Dunkirk, France, between May 29 and June 4.

British and other Allied troops wade through the water to board ships at Dunkirk, France, in 1940. About 198,000 British and 140,000 French and Belgian troops were saved during the evacuation.

THE FALL OF FRANCE

The Battle of France began on June 5. The Germans attacked along a 100-mile (160-kilometer) front from near Laon to the English Channel. They smashed through the French forces and headed for Paris. The French army fell apart. At this point Italy declared war on Britain and France.

The French government fled Paris. The Germans occupied the city on June 14. The French cabinet, defeatist and deeply divided, asked for an armistice. Marshal Philippe Pétain, the 84-year-old hero of World War I, became premier.

More than half of France was now occupied by German troops. Pétain built a fascist state with headquarters at Vichy in the unoccupied part of France. The Vichy government worked with the Germans. This was called collaboration.

Some of the French fighting forces escaped to Britain. Called the Free French, they carried on the fight against Germany under the leadership of the French general Charles de Gaulle. French partisans, also known as the Resistance, secretly supported the Free French in France.

THE BATTLE OF BRITAIN

Hitler expected that the fall of France would cause Britain to surrender. However, the British were determined to fight on. Starting in August 1940 the Germans launched mass air attacks against England. Almost daily hundreds of German planes swarmed

A national hero for his victory at the Battle of Verdun in World War I, Philippe Pétain became discredited as chief of state of the French government at Vichy in World War II.

across the English Channel from bases in occupied France to bomb England. At first the attacks targeted British ports, airfields, and radar stations. In early September, however, Hitler ordered the Luftwaffe to shift its attacks to London and other cities. These relentless bombing raids are known as the Blitz.

The German air attack was to be followed by an invasion of England. Hermann Göring, World War I air ace and commander of the German Luftwaffe, had told Hitler his planes could drive the British Royal Air Force (RAF) out of the skies. Instead, the greatly outnumbered RAF destroyed the German bombers at a crippling rate. The Battle of Britain, as the RAF defense of the country was called, was one of the most important battles in the history of the world. Never after October 1940 did Hitler seriously consider invading Britain.

EARLY STAGES OF THE WAR | 17

An aircraft spotter looks for Luftwaffe planes in the skies above London. During the German bombing raids known as the Blitz, 60,000 people were killed, 87,000 were seriously injured, and 2 million homes were destroyed.

JAPAN THREATENS IN FAR EAST

Japan was an industrialized country, but it had few natural resources. The United States was its principal supplier of raw materials prior to 1939, but the Japanese had already begun to look elsewhere.

Japanese expansion began in 1931–32 with the seizure of Manchuria, in northeastern China. In the following years Japan seized more territory bordering on Manchuria. By 1937 the Japanese had secured most of northeastern China, including Beijing, Shanghai, and Nanjing. The atrocities committed against civilians by the Japanese in their seizure of Nanjing were some of the most terrible of the war. The Chinese Nationalists under Chiang Kai-shek and the Communists under Mao Zedong put aside their civil war to oppose the Japanese, but to little avail.

Germany's conquest of the Netherlands and France left undefended the rich Netherlands Indies and French Indochina. In September Japan threatened to invade French Indochina. By this threat it gained air bases there to use in its war against China. The Chinese were isolated by Japan's seizure of their ports, roads, and railroads.

On September 27 Japan signed the Tripartite, or Axis, Pact with Germany and Italy. The pact joined the three nations in an effort to create a new world order. Their alliance would become known as the Rome-Berlin-Tokyo Axis, or the Axis Powers. Under the agreement Germany and Italy would control Europe and Japan would control eastern Asia.

EARLY STAGES OF THE WAR

THE ROLE OF THE UNITED STATES

To check Japanese expansion, the United States kept its fleet in the Pacific. It also placed economic restraints, or sanctions, on Japan, which depended on the United States for scrap iron, oil, cotton, and metals. In September 1940 the United States banned shipments of many of these materials to Japan.

The fall of France left Britain and its empire fighting alone. On September 3 the United States transferred 50 old destroyers to Britain. In return the United States got 99-year leases on sites for air and naval bases in the British possessions of Newfoundland, Bermuda, British Guiana, and the British West Indies.

The United States also went to work speeding up its rearmament. A two-ocean navy was planned. An air force of 50,000 airplanes was started. In October the nation adopted peacetime compulsory military service for the first time in its history.

THE WAR IN THE MEDITERRANEAN AND NEAR EAST

In the winter of 1940–41 Germany and Italy started a campaign against British power in the Mediterranean region. The British position in the Mediterranean was based on control of the two bottleneck passages to the sea—Gibraltar at the western end and the Suez Canal in the east.

The Axis campaign was launched against Suez. An Italian attack in North Africa was coupled with a German drive through southeastern Europe. The object was to drive the British from the eastern Mediterranean. The Italian offensive was a failure. By early 1941 almost all Mussolini's East African empire was in British hands.

Germany had more success in the Balkans. It overran Romania, Hungary, Bulgaria, Yugoslavia, and Greece. It was then able to come to Italy's aid. The British forces were driven out of Libya.

EARLY STAGES OF THE WAR | 21

German soldiers prepare to cross the Danube River from Romania into Bulgaria in 1941. Though the German campaign in the Balkans was successful, it delayed an invasion of the Soviet Union for several crucial months.

KEY FIGURES OF WORLD WAR II

THE WAR DURING 1941

Early in 1941 Britain announced that it soon would be unable to pay for the war materials it had been buying from the United States. Congress gave the president authority to lend or lease arms and supplies to countries whose defense he thought important to the security of the United States. Under the Lend-Lease Act a steady stream of planes, tanks, guns, and other war goods rolled off American assembly lines to be sent to Britain and other Allied nations. The United States became known as the Arsenal of Democracy.

Getting these supplies across the Atlantic and into the hands of British soldiers became a major problem. U.S. President Franklin D. Roosevelt announced he would take any measures necessary to ensure their delivery. On April 9 the United States took

EARLY STAGES OF THE WAR

U.S. President Franklin D. Roosevelt signs the Lend-Lease Act at the White House in 1941. The bill gave aid to Britain and to other Allied countries, such as the Soviet Union and China.

Greenland under its protection for the rest of the war. In July American troops replaced the British forces in Iceland.

On August 9, 1941, Roosevelt met with Winston Churchill on a battleship off the coast of Newfoundland. After five days of talks they issued the Atlantic Charter. Although the United States was not yet officially in the war, this document outlined the Allies' war aims and called for the "final destruction of Nazi tyranny." American and British military staffs had already agreed that in the event of a war against both Japan and Germany, the Allies would concentrate on the defeat of Germany first.

GERMANY INVADES THE SOVIET UNION

Both Germany and the Soviet Union thought of their nonaggression pact of 1939 as temporary. It gave the Soviets time to build defenses against German attack. It gave Germany peace along its eastern frontiers during the war in the west. Throughout the spring of 1941, however, there were signs that the pact might be broken.

On June 22 Germany invaded the Soviet Union. Other nations quickly took sides. Italy, Hungary, Finland, and Romania declared war on the Soviet Union. Britain pledged aid to the Soviet Union, and the United States promised war goods.

The Germans drove rapidly forward, cutting off entire Soviet armies. Despite these losses, strong resistance by the Red Army and guerrilla warfare behind the German lines slowed the German drive. As the Soviets retreated they destroyed crops, factories, railways, utility plants, and everything else that would be of value to the advancing Nazis. This is known as a "scorched earth" policy.

By December snow and cold weather had stopped the German offensive for the winter. The Soviets launched counteroffensives that drove the Germans back from the outskirts of Moscow and Leningrad (St. Petersburg).

While Germany was attacking the Soviet Union, British armies in Egypt struck at the Axis forces in Libya, driving them from Benghazi on December 25. The British then sent many of their forces to Greece to oppose the German invasion there. The British were defeated and withdrew to the island of Crete, which was later captured by German paratroopers.

JAPAN MOVES TOWARD WAR

The Japanese declared that they wanted peace, but they continued their warlike acts. In late July the United States, Britain, and the refugee Dutch government in London placed embargoes on the shipment of oil to Japan.

General Tojo Hideki became premier of Japan in October. In November he sent a special envoy to seek peace with the United States. In fact, Japan was just playing for time in which to get its armed forces into position for attack. Japan's lack of natural resources meant that it would need to win quickly. Japanese leaders were convinced that once the Americans were involved in the European war, they would be willing to negotiate a peace in the Pacific.

On November 26 American Secretary of State Cordell Hull announced that the United States would give full economic cooperation to Japan. In return he asked that Japan withdraw from China and stop collaborating with the Axis. On December 6 President Roosevelt appealed directly to the Japanese emperor, Hirohito, to work for peace. Japan rejected the American proposal.

THE ATTACK ON PEARL HARBOR

Early on the morning of December 7, 1941, Japanese submarines and carrier-launched aircraft attacked Pearl Harbor, Hawaii. The U.S. forces were completely

EARLY STAGES OF THE WAR | 27

The attack on Pearl Harbor sank two battleships and severely damaged six others. Some 190 army and navy airplanes were destroyed on the ground.

surprised. More than 2,300 Americans were killed in the two-hour attack. Eight battleships were sunk or damaged. Many cruisers and destroyers were hit. Most American planes were destroyed on the ground.

Two and a half hours after the attack at Pearl Harbor the Japanese officially declared war on the United States and Britain. The U.S. Congress declared that a state of war had existed since December 7.

CHAPTER TWO

A HARD-WON VICTORY

The entry of the United States into the war proved to be a turning point. However, victory for the Allies would come only after almost four more years of heavy fighting.

THE WAR DURING 1942

At the beginning of 1942 the Allies were on the defensive in all the theaters of war. German submarine attacks continued to sink Allied ships and their cargo more quickly than the Allies could replace them. U-boat operations had spread from the area of the British Isles into the rest of the Atlantic Ocean. This part of the war was called the Battle of the Atlantic.

In the Pacific, Guam and Wake islands had fallen to the Japanese in December 1941. The Japanese had also taken Hong Kong from the British, and much of the American fleet lay in ruins at Pearl Harbor. The Japanese continued to take new territory in the first half

KEY FIGURES OF WORLD WAR II

Germany used large numbers of diesel-electric submarines known as U-boats (short for Unterseeboot, meaning "undersea boat") against British and American shipping during World War II.

A HARD-WON VICTORY

of 1942. Filipino and American forces made heroic defensive stands at Bataan and Corregidor, but the Philippines fell in May. Also by May Singapore, the Dutch East Indies, Burma (Myanmar), and parts of New Britain and New Guinea were in Japanese hands. In northern Australia, Darwin was heavily bombed.

THE BATTLE OF MIDWAY

In June a strong invasion force of Japanese moved directly against the Hawaiian Islands. American ships, Navy planes, and Army planes from Midway Island fought a four-day battle against the invaders. The Americans lost a carrier, a destroyer, and 150 planes. The invaders, however, were completely defeated. Meanwhile a Japanese force occupied several of the Aleutian Islands.

The Battle of Midway ended serious Japanese expansion and is considered the turning point in the Pacific. U.S. Marines and Army forces attacked the

Solomon Islands in August. A month later American and Australian forces started to drive the Japanese out of New Guinea.

THE WAR IN NORTH AFRICA

The Axis forces had almost complete control of the Mediterranean Sea. Supplies for the British forces in Egypt, the Near East, and India had to be shipped around Africa. In January 1942 German General Erwin Rommel and his Afrika Korps started a new drive to seize the Suez Canal.

After losing Benghazi in January the British held the Axis forces in check until May. Then a powerful attack engulfed most of the British tank force and moved into Egypt. In July the British were finally able to stop the drive at El Alamein.

In August General Bernard L. Montgomery was named field commander of British forces in Egypt. On October 23 the British started a devastating attack from El Alamein. Rommel's tank force was routed. By November 6 the

A HARD-WON VICTORY | 33

British had driven the Axis forces from Egypt. El Alamein is considered the turning point of the war in North Africa.

British troops capture a German tank during the Battle of El Alamein. The British attack forced the Axis forces back 1,300 miles (2,100 kilometers) across the desert.

Allied forces under the command of U.S. General Dwight D. Eisenhower landed in French North Africa on November 8, 1942. They captured the strategic points in Algeria and Morocco in a few days.

The Vichy government denounced the attack, and the Nazis occupied all of France. French navy officers, however, kept the French fleet at Toulon from German use by scuttling it. The French in Africa soon ended all resistance.

THE RUSSIAN FRONT IN 1942

By the spring of 1942 the Soviet Union had regained one sixth of the territory it had lost in 1941. Then warm weather brought a new German assault. Sevastopol fell to the Germans in July. They also advanced to within 100 miles (160 kilometers) of the Caspian Sea and the important oil fields near the city of Baku. In August the Germans attacked Stalingrad (now Volgograd). The Red Army in Stalingrad was determined to fight to the last man. This bloody resistance stopped the German attack. This was the turning point of the war in Europe. In November the Soviets counterattacked and began to drive the Germans back.

THE WAR DURING 1943

The Allies won major victories in the Pacific and the Mediterranean region during 1943. On the Eastern Front, the Soviets began to push the Germans back.

A HARD-WON VICTORY

ADVANCES IN THE PACIFIC

By 1943 the Japanese were on the defensive everywhere in the Pacific. Guadalcanal in the Solomon Islands finally fell to U.S. Marines and Army forces in February 1943. This ended six months of bloody jungle warfare. During the fight for Guadalcanal a large part of the Japanese fleet was destroyed.

In the spring and summer of 1943 U.S. General Douglas MacArthur and Admiral W.F. (Bull) Halsey worked closely together. Their aim was to drive the Japanese out of eastern New Guinea, the

On August 7, 1942, the U.S. 1st Marine Division landed on Guadalcanal and seized the Japanese airfield. This was the beginning of a long battle for control of the island.

Solomons, and the Bismarck Archipelago. By early fall Allied efforts had cleared an outer ring of positions covering Australia. Meanwhile Americans and Canadians had also cleaned out Japanese forces in the Aleutians.

In November a U.S. Marine-Army force invaded the Gilbert Islands. The attack on Tarawa resulted in some of the bloodiest fighting of the war, costing the Marine Corps some 3,000 casualties.

MacArthur's troops in the southwest Pacific continued their island-hopping attack into December. By the end of 1943 Australia was no longer threatened by the Japanese.

SUCCESS IN THE MEDITERRANEAN

In February 1943 General Eisenhower was appointed commander in chief of the Allied armies in the North African theater of operations. His objective—to oust the Axis forces from North Africa—was accomplished by May.

The Allies invaded Sicily in July. On July 25 Mussolini was forced to resign as premier of Italy. He was then arrested. King Victor Emmanuel appointed Marshal Pietro Badoglio to succeed Mussolini. The British 8th Army invaded southern Italy on September 3. Badoglio's government surrendered its armed forces unconditionally on September 8. This took Italy out of the war, but the Germans, under Field Marshal Albert Kesselring, continued to fight. The Allies were forced to

A HARD-WON VICTORY

battle their way up the Italian mainland throughout the fall and early winter of 1943. Mussolini was rescued by a German commando raid and put in charge of a puppet government in northern Italy.

SOVIET COUNTERATTACK

The Soviet counterattack against the Germans gained full power by January 1943. The Soviets forced the Axis armies from Stalingrad, Kharkiv, and Smolensk. The German defeat at Kursk (July 5–August 23) was the largest tank battle of the war. By the end of the year the Soviets had reached the Polish border of 1939.

THE WAR AT SEA

The Battle of the Atlantic was fiercely fought in 1943. The Germans kept as many as 240 submarines prowling the sea lanes in wolf packs. They sank about 700 merchant ships before the Allies developed several good defenses against undersea attacks. The Allies bombed German submarine bases without letup and convoyed ships with long-range bombers. There were also major advances in radar and sonar. Another critical factor in defeating the U-boats was the British ability to read top-secret German radio communications. The British had broken the German "Enigma" code used to control the U-boats and also to send important high command messages. The resulting intelligence, code named "Ultra," was also provided to American and British commanders in France and Italy. By the end of the year the Allies had almost ended the submarine menace in the Atlantic.

THE WAR IN THE AIR

The Allies were producing enough airplanes by 1943 to carry the air war into the heart of Germany. The mass bombing of targets deep in enemy territory was called strategic bombing. The British-American bombing attacks began to take their toll on German industry.

In 1940 the RAF's Hurricane and Spitfire fighter aircraft had proved equal to German fighters such as the Messerschmitt ME-109. The first American planes were not as effective, but the later Thunderbolt (P-47) and Mustang (P-51) were excellent.

For bombers the British used Lancasters and Halifaxes, which could carry one-ton and two-ton "blockbusters." Early in the war the British made daylight

A HARD-WON VICTORY

bombing raids, but they turned to night raids after suffering crippling losses.

The American 8th Air Force preferred daylight bombing raids because targets could be hit more effectively. Americans flew in large numbers and in

The P-47 Thunderbolt, a U.S. fighter-bomber nicknamed the Jug, was known for its ability to stay in the air even after taking damage in battles.

tight formations. The planes they used were the Flying Fortress (B-17) and the Liberator (B-24).

At first the Americans suffered serious losses just as the British had. When the Mustang fighter plane was brought into the theater, however, they were able to ward off attacks by the German fighters. The Mustang could carry more fuel than other fighters and escort the bombers on their deepest raids.

AIR TRANSPORT

The Americans developed air transport on a worldwide scale during World War II. By the end of the war the U.S. Army Air Transport Command, with almost 3,000 planes, was flying a global network of 188,000 miles (303,000 kilometers) of routes. The Navy flew 420 planes over 65,000 miles (105,000 kilometers) of routes. In the China-Burma-India theater the 10th Air Force flew over the "hump" of the Himalayas, carrying supplies from India to China.

By 1943 the Allies were also using planes to carry their combat troops into action. Large transports (C-47s) carried paratroops who were dropped by parachute over their objectives. Airborne troops were also carried in gliders towed by transport planes. The Germans had pioneered the use of parachute and glider troops early in the war.

THE WAR DURING 1944

In February 1944 U.S. Admiral Chester Nimitz's forces advanced more than 2,000 miles (3,200 kilometers) from Hawaii to seize Kwajalein atoll and Enewetak in the Marshall Islands. The next advance was some 1,200 miles (1,900 kilometers) to the Marianas. By mid-August Saipan, Tinian, and Guam had fallen to the Allies. New, long-range Superfortress planes (B-29s) were used to bomb Japan.

In October General MacArthur's forces invaded the Philippines at Leyte Island. After savage fighting by land, sea, and air forces, the conquest of Leyte was complete about Christmas Day 1944.

In China, Chiang Kai-shek's forces remained on the defensive. A Japanese attack toward Changsha, begun on May 27, won control not only of a stretch of the Beijing-Hankou railroad but also of several of key airfields.

SOVIET ADVANCES

Throughout the early months of 1944 the main pressure upon the Germans was caused by Soviet attacks. One drive carried the Soviet armies to the Baltic states by spring. In the southwest they also drove deep into Ukraine.

Other drives neutralized Finland, took Minsk and Pinsk in Poland, and forced Romania to ask for peace. The Soviet Union also forced Romania to declare war on Germany on August 24. When the Soviets invaded Bulgaria in September that country also declared war on Germany. The Soviets next plunged into Yugoslavia to unite with Yugoslav partisan forces under Marshal Tito. The Yugoslav capital, Belgrade, was captured on October 20. The year ended on the Eastern Front with the Germans driven back to their own borders.

THE ITALIAN CAMPAIGN

In late 1943, following a meeting in Tehran between Roosevelt, Churchill, and Stalin, General Eisenhower was named supreme Allied commander in western Europe. Britain's General Sir Harold Alexander was made commander of the Allied forces in Italy.

An invasion force was landed at Anzio in January. Allied forces were pinned down on the beachhead, and by spring the attack looked hopeless. In May, however, a heavy attack broke through south of Cassino. The attackers joined the forces at Anzio and swept on to take Rome in June.

THE NORMANDY INVASION

Early on the morning of June 6, known as D-Day, an invasion fleet of some 7,000 ships landed American, British, and Canadian divisions on the beaches of

A HARD-WON VICTORY | 43

Normandy, France. Airborne divisions dropped behind the German lines. In the air Allies had complete command. This invasion was decisive, and the outcome of the war in Europe depended upon its success.

In the first week the Allies established beachheads between Cherbourg and the city of Caen along a 60-mile- (97-kilometer-) wide strip. Within

The Allies stormed ashore at Normandy on June 6, 1944—known as D-Day. The long-awaited invasion of Europe was known as Operation Overlord.

a week they drove about 20 miles (32 kilometers) inland. Casualties for the landing were about 15,000 out of some 150,000 engaged. The Germans never managed to mount a serious counterattack.

The British captured Caen on July 9. The Americans broke out of their beachhead positions on July 25. Armored columns headed inland, and Paris fell to the Allies on August 25. Victory seemed to be at hand, but soon the Allies outran their supply lines and German resistance increased.

THE NAZIS FIGHT BACK

The Germans began to use new weapons against England: flying robotic bombs, called V-1s, launched from bases in France, and ballistic missiles, called V-2s, launched from the Netherlands. The V-bombs injured and killed many English civilians and caused great damage.

East of the Rhine the Germans battled grimly to keep the Allies from entering Germany. In September, however, Allied troops crossed the German border east of Aachen.

As the cold, wet season advanced, the Allied drive slowed down. The Germans launched a surprise counterattack on December 16. The main attack came south of Aachen in the Ardennes. The Battle of the Bulge, as this attack was called, ended in final German defeat in this region. The year ended with the Allied forces in the west and east ready to throw their weight into the drive that would crush Nazi power.

THE WAR DURING 1945

After driving the Germans from the Ardennes the Allied armies advanced into Germany. By the end of March 1945 the Americans and British had advanced halfway across Germany.

The Germans also collapsed on other fronts. Budapest fell to the Soviets in February and Vienna in April. Mussolini was caught and shot by partisans on April 28. The next day the Germans in Italy surrendered unconditionally.

GERMANY FALLS

Despite the utter hopelessness of the German cause, Hitler remained defiant in his underground Berlin bunker. The Soviets attacked Berlin on April 21. To escape capture by the Soviets Hitler committed suicide the night of April 30.

On May 4 British General Bernard Montgomery received the surrender of the Germans in Denmark, the Netherlands, and northwestern Germany. General Alfred Jodl signed a surrender at Reims on May 7. On May 8 Churchill, Stalin, and Harry S. Truman, the new U.S. president, announced that General Wilhelm Keitel had surrendered unconditionally the day before. Now all attention turned to the Far East.

THE DEFEAT OF JAPAN

In December 1944 British General William Slim's 14th Army launched a campaign to drive the Japanese from

Burma. By May 1945 they had succeeded, recapturing Rangoon (Yangon). Chinese forces also went on the attack. By April the entire Burma Road, from Mandalay to China, was open.

Early in 1945 General MacArthur's forces in the Pacific landed an invasion force at Lingayen Gulf in Luzon, in the Philippines. Effective resistance in Manila ended in late February. It took many months, however, for the Americans to clear out the last pockets of Japanese resistance in the Philippines.

Meanwhile Admiral Nimitz's forces seized Iwo Jima and Okinawa. At Iwo Jima Marine casualties were the heaviest suffered in any island invasion, more than 20,000. During the Okinawa campaign the Navy was attacked by kamikaze (suicide) planes. The pilots of these planes deliberately flew them into American ships.

On July 26 Allied leaders met in Potsdam, Germany. They demanded that Japan immediately surrender or face utter destruction. Japan fought on.

A HARD-WON VICTORY | 47

U.S. Marines invaded Iwo Jima on February 19, 1945, and conquered it after desperate fighting on March 16. Though small, the island was home to strategically important airfields.

On August 8 the Soviet Union attacked the Japanese in Manchuria.

At this point American scientists made a significant contribution to the war effort. During the war they had developed an atomic bomb. President Truman decided to use the bomb to avoid the millions of casualties expected if the Allies had to invade Japan. On August 6 a B-29 dropped an atomic bomb on Hiroshima, Japan, a major munitions center, destroying about three fifths of the city. When the Japanese still refused to surrender, a more powerful atomic bomb was dropped on the port city of Nagasaki, leaving it in ruins. As many as 120,000 people died in these two attacks.

After the bombing of Nagasaki, Emperor Hirohito ordered the surrender of Japan. The Japanese accepted Allied terms on August 15. On September 2, 1945 (this date was September 1 in the United States), Japan formally surrendered aboard the battleship *Missouri* anchored in Tokyo Bay. General MacArthur accepted the surrender as Supreme Commander for the Allied Powers.

MacArthur immediately established military occupation of the empire. American troops went ashore to liberate war prisoners and to make certain that the Japanese complied with the terms of surrender. All Japanese military forces were disarmed and sent home. Many of Japan's war leaders were arrested and held for trial.

CHAPTER THREE

AMERICAN LEADERS

DOUGLAS MACARTHUR
(1880–1964)

Douglas MacArthur was born on January 26, 1880, on an Army reservation in Little Rock, Arkansas. His father, General Arthur MacArthur, served with distinction in the American Civil and Spanish-American wars and was military governor of the Philippines under President William McKinley.

Young MacArthur graduated from the United States Military Academy at West Point, New York, in 1903 with the highest scholastic record achieved by any cadet in 25 years. When the United States entered World War I, he helped organize the Rainbow Division and served with distinction. After the war he was appointed superintendent of West Point. Only 39 years old, he was the youngest superintendent in the history of the academy. At 50 MacArthur became chief of staff of the Army. He became the youngest full general in U.S. history.

MacArthur retired from the service in 1937, but he was recalled to active service as commander

A symbol of American determination and fighting ability, Douglas MacArthur played a major role in the ability of the United States to prepare for action in the early days of World War II.

of the U.S. forces in the Far East in July 1941. That December the Japanese bombed Pearl Harbor. They launched another attack on the Philippines, but MacArthur stood firm. Under his command 12,000 American and 35,000 Filipino troops put up fierce resistance. Besieged on the Bataan peninsula, they beat back a vastly superior Japanese invasion force.

On February 22, 1942, President Franklin D. Roosevelt sent a secret message to MacArthur commanding him to break through the Japanese lines and go to Australia. There he was to take command of Allied forces in the Southwest Pacific. MacArthur transferred his Philippine command to General Jonathan M. Wainwright. On the night of March 11, MacArthur, his wife and son, and members of his staff ran the Japanese blockade in four torpedo boats. The Philippines fell to Japan a few months later, but the Filipinos remembered his promise, "I shall return," through more than three years of Japanese occupation.

MacArthur was to keep that promise. On October 20, 1944, he landed with his forces on Leyte, one of the Philippine islands. Less than a year later, on September 2, 1945, MacArthur, as commander in chief in the Pacific, accepted Japan's surrender. He then directed the occupation of Japan.

MacArthur served in the Korean War until President Harry S. Truman relieved him of all commands on April 11, 1951. MacArthur died in Washington, D.C., on April 5, 1964.

FRANKLIN D. ROOSEVELT
(1882–1945)

Franklin Delano Roosevelt was born on January 30, 1882, at the family estate on the Hudson River near Hyde Park, New York. His father, James Roosevelt, was a wealthy landowner and railroad vice president. His mother was Sara Delano Roosevelt, of an old merchant-shipping family.

In 1910 Roosevelt was elected state senator. He became the assistant secretary of the Navy in 1913. During World War I he helped lead the Navy to victory over German sea forces. In the postwar years he helped the Germans to rebuild their country.

In the summer of 1921, Roosevelt was stricken with polio. After days of pain and fever, he was left with the aftereffects of the disease—his legs were completely and permanently paralyzed.

Roosevelt was elected governor of New York in 1928 and president of the United States

AMERICAN LEADERS | 53

Franklin D. Roosevelt, the only U.S. president to be elected four times, led the country through two of the greatest crises of the 20th century: the Great Depression and World War II.

in 1932. When he came to the White House, the United States was in the grips of the Great Depression. Millions of people had no work and no money. Roosevelt used his powers to create jobs and to help those who needed help. To do this he changed the government's role in national life.

For years Roosevelt worked to awaken the United States to the dangers of war. However, public opinion was firmly against involvement in foreign wars. The best Roosevelt could do was to build up American defenses and provide supplies and economic support to the Allies.

After the Japanese struck Pearl Harbor in 1941, Congress passed the First and Second War Powers Acts and other laws to give Roosevelt full authority. He had control over farming, manufacturing, labor, prices, wages, transportation, and allotment of raw materials. In turn he gave these powers to the right people, boards, or departments. Many war agencies were set up. Shifting and changing as needed, they brought nearly every activity of the country under government direction.

Throughout the course of the war, Roosevelt attended several conferences with other Allied leaders. One of the most important took place at Yalta in Crimea in February 1945. There Roosevelt, British Prime Minister Winston Churchill, and Soviet Premier Joseph Stalin discussed final war plans and peace questions.

On the morning of April 12, 1945, Roosevelt was busy signing documents and studying state papers. Suddenly he slumped in his chair. He had suffered a cerebral hemorrhage. Death came swiftly. That evening Vice President Harry S. Truman was sworn in as president.

HARRY S. TRUMAN
(1884–1972)

Harry S. Truman was born on May 8, 1884, in Lamar, Missouri. He was the son of John Anderson Truman, a cattle trader, and Martha Young Truman. Shortly after Harry's birth, the Truman family moved to nearby Independence, Missouri. There he attended grade school and high school.

Truman was a farmer when the United States entered World War I in 1917. As a member of the Missouri National Guard, he was sent overseas and served in France.

In 1934 Truman was elected to the U.S. Senate. In 1940 he toured the country in his own car at his own expense to observe the progress of World War II work. The irregularities he saw during his 30,000-mile (48,000-kilometer) tour prompted him to ask the Senate to create the Committee Investigating the National Defense Program, commonly called the Truman Committee. It helped to correct many cases of mismanagement, waste, and negligence in the war effort.

The 1944 Democratic National Convention was split over whom to nominate for vice president. The deadlock was broken by naming Truman as the compromise candidate. When Franklin D. Roosevelt

Harry S. Truman led the United States through the last months of World War II. He also played a major role in shaping how the country and world looked after the war.

won a fourth term, Truman became the vice president. In that role Truman had little to do with shaping America's policies at home or abroad. Roosevelt seldom consulted with him. As a result, when Roosevelt suddenly died, Truman, as president, faced many problems. Presidential aides and others did their best to help him, and Truman learned quickly.

Two weeks after he became president, Truman learned of the top-secret project to develop an atomic bomb. On July 16, 1945, he was told a successful atom bomb test had been made at Los Alamos, New Mexico. Truman consulted with his aides to decide whether the bomb should be used against Japan. An invasion of Japan was being planned. They estimated that if the bomb worked it would save a quarter of a million American lives. Truman suggested that the United States warn Japan that, if it did not surrender, the bomb would be used. Japan refused to yield. U.S. planes dropped atomic bombs on the cities of Hiroshima (August 6) and Nagasaki (August 9). On August 15 Japan surrendered.

After the war Truman helped the United States join the United Nations, an international peace organization. He also introduced the Truman Doctrine, which said that the United States would fight the spread of communism.

In 1948 Truman approved the Marshall Plan. Under the plan the United States sent billions of dollars to help rebuild Europe. By strengthening the economies of western Europe, the plan helped to prevent communism from spreading there.

Truman made another stand against communism in 1950, sending U.S. troops to repel communist North Korea's invasion of South Korea. The Korean War dragged on inconclusively past the end of Truman's presidency in 1953. Truman died in Kansas City, Missouri, on December 26, 1972.

CHESTER W. NIMITZ
(1885–1966)

Chester William Nimitz was born in Fredericksburg, Texas, on February 24, 1885. He graduated from the United States Naval Academy in 1905. During World War I he was chief of staff to the commander of the U.S. Atlantic submarine fleet. After the war he furthered his education and held a variety of posts at sea and on shore. By World War II he had reached the rank of admiral.

After the Japanese attack on Pearl Harbor in December 1941, Nimitz became commander in chief of the Pacific Fleet. In this position, both land and sea forces came under his authority. In June 1942 he directed the decisive U.S. victory over Japan at the Battle of Midway. In the years that followed, the historic battles of the Solomon Islands (1942–43), the Gilbert Islands (1943), the Marshalls, Marianas, Palaus, and Philippines (1944), and Iwo Jima and Okinawa (1945) were fought under his direction.

The formal Japanese surrender was signed aboard Nimitz's flagship, the USS *Missouri*, in Tokyo Bay in September 1945. In December 1944 he had

Chester W. Nimitz served as commander of all U.S. land and sea forces in the Pacific during World War II. He was one of the U.S. Navy's foremost administrators and strategists.

been promoted to the U.S. Navy's newest and highest rank—that of fleet admiral. After the war Nimitz served as chief of naval operations from 1945 to 1947. He died near San Francisco, California, on February 20, 1966.

GEORGE PATTON
(1885–1945)

George Smith Patton, Jr., was born on the family ranch in San Gabriel, California, on November 11, 1885. In high school he was an expert horseman, fencer, and swimmer. At the age of 18 he entered Virginia Military Institute, but after a year he transferred to the United States Military Academy at West Point, New York. He graduated in 1909 as a cavalry officer.

At the 1912 Olympic Games in Stockholm, Sweden, Patton placed fifth as the U.S. representative in the modern pentathlon. During World War I he organized a training center for American tank crews in France. Later he commanded a tank corps in the St-Mihiel and Meuse-Argonne offensives. Injured during the war, he was decorated for his accomplishments.

In World War II Patton injected the spirit of the cavalry into mechanized warfare. His quick tank thrusts knifed through the enemy lines, upsetting the enemy's defensive strategy. These slashing attacks brought spectacular victories in North Africa and Sicily. But it was his 1944 drive across Europe into Germany that won Patton his greatest fame. In less than 10 months his armor

George Patton's hard-driving leadership helped make him the foremost tank specialist of World War II. His relentless attacks won him the nickname Old Blood and Guts.

and infantry roared through France, Belgium, Luxembourg, Germany, Austria, and Czechoslovakia.

After the war, during the period of occupation, Patton was involved for a time in the military governorship of Bavaria. The qualities of ruthlessness and inflexibility that had made him a successful general did not prove useful in this work. His outspoken opposition to the official policy of denazification (the removal from power of Nazi Party members) ultimately forced his superiors to relieve him of any real responsibility.

On December 9, 1945, Patton was injured in an automobile accident near Mannheim, Germany. He was taken to a hospital in Heidelberg, where he died on December 21.

DWIGHT D. EISENHOWER
(1890–1969)

Dwight David Eisenhower was born in Denison, Texas, on October 14, 1890. Two years later his family moved to Abilene, Kansas. During his school days young Dwight was called Ike by his friends. The nickname would stay with him throughout his life.

Eisenhower attended the United States Military Academy at West Point, New York. He commanded a training center for tank crews during World War I. After the war he had assignments in the United States, the Panama Canal Zone, and Europe. In the 1930s he trained pilots in the Philippines.

Eisenhower returned to the United States in 1940, shortly after the start of World War II. The war

During World War II Dwight D. Eisenhower became one of the most successful military commanders in history. He would later be elected the 34th president of the United States.

brought him promotions to colonel and brigadier general in 1941 and to major general and lieutenant general in 1942. In July 1942 Army Chief of Staff General George C. Marshall appointed Eisenhower to take over planning for the invasion of North Africa.

In this position Eisenhower showed great talent for combining officers of different countries into a single team. He also proved he knew how to solve both military and political problems on an international scale. Eisenhower commanded the U.S. forces in the invasion of North Africa on November 8, 1942, and soon became commander in chief of the whole operation. In February 1943 he was promoted to four-star general. During that year he launched successful attacks on Tunisia, Sicily, and Italy.

In December 1943 Eisenhower was appointed supreme commander of the Allied Expeditionary Forces, placing him in charge of the forthcoming invasion of France. His forces landed in Normandy on June 6, 1944, in the greatest amphibious operation in history. By the spring of 1945 the Allies had driven through the heart of Germany. The Nazis surrendered on May 8. Meanwhile Eisenhower had received the highest U.S. military rank, five-star general, in December 1944.

Eisenhower went on to win two terms as president, in 1952 and 1956. His presidency was a period of growth and prosperity in the United States. When Eisenhower left office, Congress restored his rank as general of the Army. He returned to his farm in Gettysburg, Pennsylvania, and devoted much of his time to writing his memoirs. Eisenhower died of heart failure on March 28, 1969.

OMAR NELSON BRADLEY
(1893–1981)

Omar Nelson Bradley was born on February 12, 1893, in Clark, Missouri. He graduated from the United States Military Academy at West Point, New York, in 1915. He taught at West Point for two separate terms before being transferred to the general staff in Washington, D.C.

Bradley's first combat duties in World War II were in North Africa, where he commanded the victorious drive of the U.S. 2nd Corps into Tunisia. He then led his troops in the Sicilian invasion of 1943. Later that year he was transferred to England and given command of the 1st Army in preparation for the Normandy landing of 1944. He was next given command of the 12th Army Group, which combined troops of the 1st, 3rd, 9th, and 15th armies; it was the largest force ever placed under an American group commander. The 12th Army Group successfully carried on operations in France, Luxembourg, Belgium, the Netherlands, Germany, and Czechoslovakia until the end of the war.

In 1950 Bradley was raised to the rank of general. He retired from the service in 1953. He died in New York City on April 8, 1981.

CHAPTER FOUR

OTHER ALLIED LEADERS

WINSTON CHURCHILL
(1874–1965)

Winston Leonard Spencer Churchill was born in England on November 30, 1874, at Blenheim Palace, in the estate of the dukes of Marlborough. His father was Lord Randolph Churchill, the third son of the seventh duke. His mother, Jennie Jerome, had been a New York society beauty.

When he was 16, Churchill entered Sandhurst, a historic British military college. There he excelled in studies of tactics and fortifications and graduated 20th in a class of 130. After Sandhurst he served in the British Army. He also read widely and began to write. He left the Army in 1899. After unsuccessfully standing for Parliament, he became a war correspondent during the South African War.

Upon his return to England, Churchill was elected to Parliament. His enormous energy carried him through a succession of offices. In 1911 he was made first lord of the admiralty. He worked hard to reorganize the navy. When World

Winston Churchill rose through a stormy career to become an internationally respected statesman during World War II. He was one of Britain's greatest prime ministers.

War I broke out in 1914, Churchill's efficient navy became England's first powerful weapon against Germany.

On September 3, 1939, two days after Germany's invasion of Poland, Britain was again at war. On May 10, 1940, Prime Minister Neville Chamberlain was forced to resign. Churchill succeeded him. When Churchill took office, the armed might of Germany was sweeping Europe. Yet Churchill stood firm before the British people and declared, "I have nothing to offer but blood, toil, tears, and sweat." He promised "to wage war against a monstrous tyranny, never surpassed in the dark, lamentable catalogue of human crime." His thundering defiance and courage heartened Britain, and his two fingers raised in the "V for Victory" sign became an international symbol for determination and hope.

Before the United States entered the war, Churchill obtained American aid and met with U.S. President Franklin D. Roosevelt in 1941 to draw up the Atlantic Charter. Later he helped plan overall Allied strategy. Although Churchill held that international communism was a threat to peace, he worked with Soviet Premier Joseph Stalin for the defeat of the Nazis.

Britain's Labour-Conservative coalition government dissolved soon after the war ended in Europe. The Labour Party won the general election of 1945, forcing Churchill's resignation as prime minister.

In 1951 Churchill was again chosen prime minister of Britain; he resigned in 1955. In 1953 he was knighted by Queen Elizabeth II and received the

Nobel Prize for Literature. By an act of Congress, Churchill was made an honorary citizen of the United States in 1963.

Churchill died in London on January 24, 1965. He received a state funeral, the first for a British commoner since 1898.

JOSEPH STALIN
(1879–1953)

Joseph Stalin was born in Gori, a village in Georgia, then part of the Russian Empire, in December 1878. He attended Tiflis Theological Seminary to be educated for the priesthood, but he was more interested in communism than in theology. The seminary expelled him in 1899 for revolutionary activity. He then became a paid agitator, trying to incite revolt against the tsar. From 1902 to 1913 he was arrested seven times for revolutionary activity, undergoing repeated imprisonment and exile.

In 1903 Russia's Social Democratic Party split into two factions. Stalin joined the more militant faction, the Bolsheviks. It was headed by Vladimir Lenin. During the civil war of 1918–20, which followed the Russian Revolution of 1917, Stalin served as political commissar with Bolshevik armies on several fronts. He showed exceptional ability as a strategist and tactician.

In 1922 Stalin became Secretary General of the Central Committee of the Communist Party, and he methodically assumed increasing power. In 1925, a

Though he transformed the Soviet Union into a major world power, Joseph Stalin was also one of the most ruthless dictators of modern times.

OTHER ALLIED LEADERS | 71

year after Lenin's death, Stalin forced his rival Leon Trotsky to resign as war minister, and in 1929 he expelled him from the Soviet Union. Stalin was then supreme ruler. In the following years he continued to deal brutally with the opposition. His political victims were numbered in the tens of millions.

In August 1939 Stalin startled the world when he brought the Soviet Union into a nonaggression pact with Nazi Germany. One month later Germany invaded Poland, starting World War II. The nonaggression pact permitted the Soviets to annex eastern Poland, Estonia, Latvia, Lithuania, and parts of Romania as well as attack Finland—all without German opposition. Stalin extended Soviet borders into outlying buffer areas.

In May 1941 Stalin made himself premier of the Soviet Union. In June the Soviet Union was invaded by Germany. Stalin took command of the army and reorganized industry.

In high-level meetings in 1943 at Tehran, Iran, and early in 1945 at Yalta, Ukraine, Stalin issued inflexible terms to his allies, Prime Minister Winston Churchill of Britain and President Franklin Roosevelt of the United States. Later in 1945, at Potsdam, Germany, Stalin made a pact with U.S. President Harry Truman on the reconstruction of defeated Germany. He then defiantly broke the terms of the accord.

After the war's end, Stalin seemed to be determined to make the Soviet Union dominant in Europe and to impose communism on the world. Through purges and other relentless measures, he forced communist governments on eastern Europe.

Stalin died suddenly on March 5, 1953, in Moscow. His embalmed body was entombed alongside that of Lenin in Moscow's Red Square.

CHIANG KAI-SHEK
(1887–1975)

Chiang Kai-shek was born on October 31, 1887, in China's Zhejiang Province. He trained for a military career from a young age, first in northern China and then in Tokyo, Japan. In Japan Chiang was attracted to the teachings of the exiled Chinese revolutionary leader Sun Yat-sen. Sun and his followers wanted to overthrow the Manchus, who had controlled China since the 17th century, and to establish a republic. In 1911 Chiang returned to China and took part in the revolt that accomplished that goal.

In the years that followed, various leaders and warlords struggled for power in the country. Chiang rose to power in the Kuomintang (Nationalist Party). In 1926 he took command of the revolutionary army and began advancing north, with Beijing, capital of the weak republic, as his goal. In 1928 Chiang's army entered Beijing and, as chief of the Kuomintang, he became the head of the Republic of China.

China, however, was still deeply divided. For years Chiang battled insurgent regional commanders and armed communist forces. When Japan invaded Manchuria in 1931, Chiang offered no resistance, as he believed China still too weak to

As the leader of the Republic of China, first on the Asian mainland and later on the island of Taiwan, Chiang Kai-shek became one of the most controversial men of his time.

risk a war. Widespread criticism of his policy forced him to resign as head of the nation, but he continued as commander of the army.

When Japan again invaded China in an undeclared war, Chiang was forced to form a temporary alliance with the communists. His forces kept most of China free of Japanese control and managed to move industries and schools to the interior. After the Allied forces declared war against Japan during World War II, Chiang became Allied commander in China. He became China's president in 1943. China received economic aid from the United States, but Chiang did not push economic or political reforms. Much of his Nationalist government was corrupt, and inflation brought increasing hardship to the masses.

Chiang did not actively resist the Japanese during World War II, counting on the United States to win the war and wishing to preserve his own armies for future battles with the communists. It is thought that this strategy cost him the support of many Chinese people and demoralized his own troops. As a result, when fighting between the communists and Chiang's forces resumed at the end of the war, the Chinese communists advanced steadily. By 1949 they had won the entire mainland and established the People's Republic of China. Chiang escaped to the island of Taiwan and set up a government there called the Republic of China. Chiang remained president of the Republic of China until his death on April 5, 1975.

BERNARD MONTGOMERY
(1887–1976)

Bernard Law Montgomery was born on November 17, 1887, in London, England. In 1908 he graduated from Sandhurst, the British officers' school. In World War I he was wounded twice. Early in World War II he led a division in France.

In August 1942 Montgomery was named commander of the British 8th Army in North Africa. He forced Erwin Rommel out of Egypt in the Battle of El-Alamein and pursued the Germans to their surrender in Tunisia in May 1943. He then led the 8th in the Allied invasions of Sicily and Italy.

Following his Mediterranean service Montgomery commanded all Allied ground forces in the June 1944 invasion of France. After the

Bernard Montgomery commanded the British 8th Army's triumphant sweep across North Africa and its invasion of Sicily and Italy.

breakthrough at the base of the Cherbourg peninsula, he commanded the armies that swept across northern France into Belgium and the Netherlands. He was made chief of the British Imperial Staff in 1946 and NATO chief of five western European countries in 1948. From 1951 to 1958 he was deputy commander of the NATO forces in Europe. Montgomery died in Hampshire, England, on March 25, 1976.

CHARLES DE GAULLE
(1890–1970)

Charles-André-Joseph-Marie de Gaulle was born on November 22, 1890, at Lille, in northern France. In 1911 he graduated near the head of his class from the prestigious military school at St-Cyr and became a second lieutenant in the infantry. He served in World War I and endured more than two years as a prisoner of war under the Germans.

When Germany invaded France in 1940, de Gaulle was made a brigadier general and given command of an armored division. France failed to check the German advance, and Vice Premier Philippe Pétain signed a truce with Adolf Hitler.

De Gaulle flew to London for a series of conferences with British Prime Minister Winston Churchill. While there, de Gaulle encouraged the French to keep fighting the Germans, declaring in a radio broadcast, "France has lost a battle, but she has not lost the war." From his London base, he took control of the newly formed Free French resistance movement. After the

Throughout his career as a military leader and statesman, Charles de Gaulle was guided by a belief in the greatness of France.

American invasion of North Africa he joined General Henri Giraud in Algiers to serve as copresident of the French Committee of National Liberation. De Gaulle later became sole president of the committee and chief of the Free French armed forces. He returned to Paris in 1944 on the heels of the retreating Germans.

Appointed president of the newly established French provisional government, de Gaulle tried to unite France's many political parties into a strong national administration. His proposed constitutional reforms met with increasing hostility from the National Assembly, and in 1946 he resigned. In 1958 he returned to power, thanks in part to a political crisis brought on by the Algerian War of Independence. He continued to lead France until 1969, when he retired to his home at Colombey-les-Deux-Églises. He died there on November 9, 1970.

GEORGI KONSTANTINOVICH ZHUKOV
(1896–1974)

Georgi Konstantinovich Zhukov was born on December 1 (November 19 on the calendar used then), 1896, near Kaluga, Russia. He saw service in World War I, and after the Russian Revolution of 1917 he joined the Red Army. He rose steadily through the ranks, serving as head of Soviet forces in the Chinese border region and as chief of staff

Georgi Konstantinovich Zhukov was the Soviet Union's most acclaimed military commander of World War II. He was also the first military figure to be elected to the Presidium of the Communist Party.

of the Soviet army in the Winter War against Finland (1939–40). In January 1941 he was appointed chief of staff of the Red Army.

After the Germans invaded Russia in June 1941, Zhukov organized the defense of Leningrad (St. Petersburg) and was then appointed commander in chief of the Western Front. In August 1942 he was named first deputy commander in chief of Soviet armed forces. Zhukov became the chief member of Joseph Stalin's personal supreme headquarters and figured prominently in the planning or execution of almost every major engagement of the war. In 1943 he was named a marshal of the Soviet Union. He personally commanded the final assault on Berlin in April 1945 and then remained in Germany as commander of the Soviet occupation force. On May 8, 1945, he represented the Soviet Union at Germany's formal surrender.

Upon Zhukov's return to Moscow in 1946, his great popularity apparently caused him to be regarded as a potential threat by Stalin. The Soviet leader relegated him to minor duties. Only after Stalin's death did Zhukov return to prominence. In 1955 he became minister of defense and was elected an alternate member of the Presidium. However, his persistent efforts to reduce the Communist Party's control of the army led to his dismissal as minister of defense by Nikita Khrushchev in 1957. Zhukov was restored to favor after Khrushchev's downfall in 1964 and was awarded the Order of Lenin in 1966. He died in Moscow on June 18, 1974.

LOUIS MOUNTBATTEN
(1900–79)

Louis Francis Albert Victor Nicholas, prince of Battenberg, was born on June 25, 1900, in Windsor, England. The family name was changed to Mountbatten in 1917. In 1913 Mountbatten entered the Royal Navy, and in 1921 he became aide-de-camp to the prince of Wales.

In 1932 Mountbatten was promoted to captain. At the outbreak of World War II he commanded the destroyer *Kelly*, which was torpedoed several times. From 1943 to 1946 he served as supreme allied commander for Southeast Asia. Although many hailed him as a war hero, opponents claimed he endangered his men unnecessarily.

After the war Mountbatten was named viceroy of India (March to August 1947). He supervised the transfer of government from British to Indian rule. In later years he held Britain's highest military defense leaderships and served as governor and then lord lieutenant of the Isle of Wight. He was killed at Donegal Bay, Ireland, on August 27, 1979, by an Irish Republican Army bomb planted on his fishing boat.

CHAPTER FIVE

AXIS LEADERS

BENITO MUSSOLINI
(1883–1945)

Benito Mussolini was born in Dovia di Predappio, Italy, on July 29, 1883. A restless, disobedient child, he grew up a bully. He became a Socialist in his teens and worked, often as a schoolmaster, to spread the party doctrine.

World War I changed Mussolini. Once a reformer, he became a worshiper of power. Unlike most of the Socialists, he advocated Italy's entry into the war on the Allied side. His views got him expelled from the Socialist Party. Mussolini went to fight in the war.

During the chaos that gripped Italy after the war, Mussolini's influence grew swiftly. Into an army of supporters who wore black shirts (the symbolic uniform of anarchists) he recruited discontented Socialists, veterans, the unemployed—all the dissidents who believed that only a ruthless dictator could revitalize Italy. The new movement was called fascism. By 1922 crowds of peasants were spellbound by Mussolini's magnetism and oratory, and

AXIS LEADERS 83

As prime minister of Italy from 1922 to 1943, Benito Mussolini made the country into a dictatorship and allowed no one to question his power.

his backers were powerful enough to force King Victor Emmanuel III to bow before a fascist march on Rome to seize the government. The king named Mussolini prime minister, Italy's youngest ever. He then became dictator and was called *Il Duce* (The Leader).

As dictator, Mussolini had the power to make all decisions. He built roads, harnessed rivers, increased production, and ran the trains on time. He tried to colonize Eritrea and Libya on a grand scale. In defiance of the League of Nations he invaded Ethiopia in 1935 and seized Albania in 1939. He boasted that he was regaining the glory and prestige of ancient Rome.

Mussolini's apparent triumphs encouraged Adolf Hitler to organize Germany on the fascist pattern. They created a Rome-Berlin Axis of totalitarianism, but Mussolini became Hitler's pawn. Meanwhile his harsh rule had made enemies at home, and his international arrogance had helped pave the way to World War II. His army proved ineffectual, and German troops occupied Italy. After the Allies invaded Sicily in 1943, Mussolini was forced to resign. Rescued from prison by German troops, he set up a puppet rule for northern Italy, which was still under German control. In disguise he tried to escape from the Allied advance, but he and his mistress, Clara Petacci, were shot near Como by Italian partisans on April 28, 1945. Their bodies were exhibited to jeering crowds in the streets of Milan.

YAMAMOTO ISOROKU
(1884–1943)

Yamamoto Isoroku was born in Nagaoka, Japan, on April 4, 1884. He graduated from Japan's naval academy in 1904 and fought as an ensign in the Russo-Japanese War (1904–05). He served at sea for several years and graduated from the Naval War College in 1916. In 1919 he went to the United States to

Yamamoto Isoroku was Japan's most prominent naval officer during World War II and an early advocate of combined sea and air power. He planned and led the attack on Pearl Harbor.

study at Harvard University. He later served as naval attaché in Washington, D.C. As Japanese delegate to the London Naval Conference of 1935, he opposed restrictions on the size of the Japanese navy. He became commander in chief of the combined fleet in August 1941.

Unlike other Japanese military leaders, Yamamoto was opposed to war with the United States. For this reason he opposed signing the Tripartite Pact with Germany and Italy in 1940. Loyally following his country's war plans, however, he insisted that the American fleet at Pearl Harbor had to be destroyed if Japan was to have a free hand in the Pacific. His later campaigns in the Midway and Solomon islands were less successful. He was killed on April 18, 1943, when his airplane was shot down over the Solomon Islands.

TOJO HIDEKI
(1884–1948)

Tojo Hideki was born on December 30, 1884, in Tokyo, Japan. A graduate of the Imperial Military Academy and the Military Staff College, Tojo served briefly as military attaché in Japan's embassy in Berlin after World War I. He was an esteemed administrator and skillful field commander and became noted as a stern disciplinarian. In 1937 he was named chief of staff of the Kwantung Army in Manchuria. He returned to Tokyo in 1938 as vice

Soldier and statesman Tojo Hideki was prime minister of Japan during most of the Pacific theater portion of World War II.

minister of war and was one of the leading advocates of Japan's Tripartite Pact with Germany and Italy (1940). In July 1940 he was appointed minister of war in the cabinet of Prime Minister Prince Konoe Fumimaro. Tojo succeeded Konoe as prime minister on October 18, 1941, and pledged his government to a Greater East Asia program, a "New Order in Asia." He retained control of the Ministry of War and was also minister of commerce and industry from 1943.

A hardworking and efficient bureaucrat, Tojo was also one of the most aggressive militarists in the Japanese leadership. He led his country's war efforts after the attack on the U.S. base at Pearl Harbor on December 7, 1941, and under his direction smashing victories were initially scored throughout Southeast Asia and the western Pacific region. After a series of Japanese military reversals in the Pacific, Tojo assumed virtual dictatorial powers, taking over the post of the chief of the General Staff. The successful Allied invasion of the Mariana Islands so weakened his government, however, that he was removed as chief of staff on July 16, 1944, and on July 18 he and his entire cabinet announced their resignation. Four days later he was succeeded as prime minister by Koiso Kuniaki. Tojo spent the remainder of the war in the military reserve, effectively banned from power.

On April 29, 1946, Tojo was indicted for war crimes before the International Military Tribunal for the Far East in Tokyo. After being found guilty he was hanged on December 23, 1948.

ADOLF HITLER
(1889–1945)

Adolf Hitler was born on April 20, 1889, in Braunau am Inn, Austria, of German descent. He hoped to be an artist, but failure dogged him. As he struggled with poverty in Austria, he looked longingly across the border at powerful Germany. In 1912 he left Vienna for Munich, Germany.

Hitler fought in the German army in World War I. He joined the German Workers' Party in 1919 and quickly rose to become a leader of the group. In 1920 Hitler changed the party's name to Nationalsozialistische Deutsche Arbeiterpartei (National Socialist German Workers' Party), abbreviated to Nazi.

When the Great Depression plunged Germany into poverty and unemployment, the Nazis began to gain votes. Also aiding their rise was Germany's bitterness over its defeat in World War I and the harsh conditions of the Treaty of Versailles.

In 1933 Hitler persuaded President Paul von Hindenburg to appoint him chancellor of Germany. Once in power, Hitler established an absolute dictatorship. The Nazis began persecuting German Jews. Jewish businesses were boycotted, and books written by Jews were burned. The Nürnberg Laws of 1935 deprived Jews of German citizenship. In November 1938 in Kristallnacht ("Night of Broken Glass"), the Nazis destroyed or damaged Jewish synagogues and businesses throughout Germany and sent some 30,000 Jewish men to concentration camps.

The rise of Adolf Hitler to the position of dictator of Germany is the story of a frenzied ambition that plunged the world into the worst war in history.

Hitler devoted most of his attention to his aggressive foreign policy. He sought to take over territory outside Germany where people of German ancestry lived, and he also wanted to expand Germany farther to the east. In violation of the Treaty of Versailles, he secretly built up Germany's armed forces. His invasion of Poland on September 1, 1939, triggered World War II.

Hitler took charge of Germany's war strategy from the first. On the whole his campaign in western Europe was astonishingly successful. In 1940 Germany rapidly conquered Norway, Denmark, Belgium, the Netherlands, and France. In June 1941 Hitler launched a massive surprise attack against the Soviet Union. The Germans reached the outskirts of Moscow before Soviet counterattacks and severe winter weather halted the advance.

Meanwhile, the Nazis had begun the Holocaust, the mass murder of Jews and other groups, including Roma (Gypsies) and homosexuals. At first Hitler had wanted to expel the Jews from the German empire he was creating. Starting in 1941, he sought instead to exterminate the Jews. Special German mobile killing units rounded up and murdered Jews and others throughout the conquered territories of Europe. From 1942 the Jews in all areas controlled by the Nazis were sent to concentration and extermination camps, where they were either forced into slave labor or killed. Ultimately, the Nazis killed an estimated six million Jews and millions of others.

Allied victories in 1942–43 made the chances of German victory seem increasingly unlikely. Within

Germany, desperate officers and anti-Nazi civilians were ready to remove Hitler and negotiate a peace. Several attempts to assassinate Hitler were planned in 1943–44.

In 1945 Hitler finally accepted the inevitability of defeat in the war, and he prepared to commit suicide. First, he married his longtime mistress, Eva Braun, at midnight on April 28–29, 1945. On April 30, in his bunker in Berlin, he shot himself, and Braun took poison. As Hitler had instructed, their bodies were burned.

ERWIN ROMMEL
(1891–1944)

Erwin Johannes Eugen Rommel was born on November 15, 1891, in Heidenheim an der Brenz, Germany. At 19 he enlisted in the 124th Württemberg Infantry Regiment as a cadet. He saw service in World War I, in which he showed promise of great leadership ability.

In 1938 Rommel was appointed commandant of an officers' school near Vienna, Austria. When World War II began he was commanding troops protecting Adolf Hitler's headquarters. In February 1940 he was put in charge of his first panzer division (armored unit) and readily grasped the offensive possibilities of mechanized and armored troops. A year later he became commander of German forces in North Africa. He won the nickname the Desert

Fox for his brilliant leadership of the Afrika Korps. He had an unbroken string of successes until he was defeated by much larger forces commanded by General Bernard Montgomery at the Battle of El Alamein in Egypt in October 1942.

Rommel was ordered home in 1943. By this time he had become convinced that Germany would lose the war. He soon became involved in the plot to oust Hitler from leadership. The plot failed, and Hitler learned of Rommel's complicity. Because of his military reputation Rommel was allowed to commit suicide by poison on October 14, 1944.

HERMANN GÖRING
(1893–1946)

Hermann Göring was born on January 12, 1893, in Rosenheim, Germany. He was brought up near Nuremberg, in the small castle of Veldenstein. Trained for an army career, Göring received his commission in 1912 and served with distinction during World War I.

Göring met Adolf Hitler in 1921 and joined the small Nazi Party late in 1922. As a former officer, Göring was given command of Hitler's Storm Troopers (the SA), a paramilitary organization whose methods included violent intimidation. Göring took part in the abortive Beer Hall (Munich) Putsch of November 1923, in which Hitler tried to seize power prematurely.

As a leader of the Nazi Party, Hermann Göring became one of the primary architects of the Nazi police state in Germany during World War II.

Göring was elected to the Reichstag in 1928 and became its president in 1932. He helped bring Hitler to power as chancellor. During the rest of the decade, Göring held a series of other offices that he used to establish such elements of the Nazi state as the Gestapo (secret police) and the concentration camps for the "corrective treatment" of difficult opponents. He also became the commissioner for aviation and the head of the newly developed German air force, the Luftwaffe. In 1934 Göring ceded his position as security chief to Heinrich Himmler, thus ridding himself of responsibility for the Gestapo and the concentration camps.

It was Göring's Luftwaffe that helped conduct the blitzkrieg ("lightning war") that smashed Polish resistance and weakened country after country as Hitler's campaigns progressed. But Göring was not capable of influencing Hitler's preference for the production of bombers rather than fighter planes. As a result, the Luftwaffe's capacity for defense declined as Hitler's battlefronts extended from northern Europe to the Mediterranean and North Africa, and Göring lost face when the Luftwaffe failed to win the Battle of Britain or to prevent the Allied bombing of Germany. On the plea of ill health, Göring retired—as much as Hitler would let him.

After Hitler's suicide, Göring surrendered himself to the Americans. He was tried as a war criminal, found guilty, and sentenced to death. On October 15, 1946, the night his execution was ordered, he took poison and died in his cell at Nuremberg.

HIROHITO
(1901–89)

Michinomiya Hirohito was born at Aoyama Palace in Tokyo, Japan, on April 29, 1901. He received his early education at the Peers' School and later attended the Crown Prince's Institute. He studied marine biology, on which he later wrote several books based on research he had done in Sagami Bay. In 1921 he paid a visit to Europe, the first Japanese crown prince to do so. When he returned home he was named prince regent to rule in place of his father, who had retired because of mental illness. Following his father's death on December 25, 1926, Hirohito became emperor of Japan.

The first 20 years of Hirohito's reign were tumultuous. By the time he became emperor, the military was already in firm control of policy and impelling Japan into a major war. The emperor had grave misgivings about any war with the United States and tried vainly to restrain the army and navy chiefs. In 1945, when Japan was nearing defeat, opinion was divided between those who favored surrender and those who wanted to carry on the war to the bitter end. Hirohito sided with those urging peace. On August 15, 1945, he broadcast on radio his country's surrender.

After the war, there were changes in Hirohito's position. He renounced his divinity. The constitution that had given the emperor supreme authority was rewritten. The new constitution

The role of the emperor is so significant in Japanese society that, when Japan surrendered in World War II, Hirohito was allowed to retain his position and title.

vested sovereignty in the people, and the emperor was designated "symbol of the State and of the unity of the people." He became more accessible, making personal appearances and permitting publication of pictures and stories of himself and his family. In 1959 he permitted his son, Crown Prince Akihito, to marry a commoner. Hirohito died on January 7, 1989, after a long illness.

CONCLUSION

Even though World War II took place in the middle of the last century, you still hear people talking about the battles that raged and the leaders who made their names in the war. There are thousands of books on the military history of World War II and the skilled military commanders whose tactics helped determine the course of the war. Movies about the war continue to be popular, too.

The events of World War II cemented the legacies of the world leaders at the center of the conflict. Hitler's name has become a byword for brutality. It is unlikely that his reputation as the incarnation of evil will ever change. On the other hand, people continue to be inspired by the rousing speeches that Winston Churchill and Franklin D. Roosevelt gave to the British and American people, preparing them for the long, hard fight.

GLOSSARY

amphibious operation A military attack launched from the sea that involves landing forces on the shore.

appeasement Pacifying an aggressor by concessions, usually at the sacrifice of principles.

armistice A temporary suspension of hostilities by agreement between the opponents.

atrocity A very cruel and terrible act.

ballistic missile A weapon that is shot through the sky over a great distance and then falls to the ground and explodes.

blockade An act of war in which one country uses ships to stop people or supplies from entering or leaving another country.

campaign A connected series of military operations forming a distinct phase of a war.

communism A way of organizing a society in which the government owns the things that are used to make and transport products (such as land, oil, factories, ships, etc.) and there is no privately owned property.

compulsory Required by a law or rule.

counteroffensive An attack made in order to defend against an enemy or opponent.

dictator A person who rules a country with total authority and often in a cruel or brutal way.

GLOSSARY

fascism A form of government ruled by a dictator who controls the lives of the people and in which people are not allowed to disagree with the government.

fortification A military defense built to protect a place against attacks.

front A zone of conflict between armies.

guerrilla warfare Attacks carried out by small groups of soldiers who do not belong to a regular army and who fight in a war as an independent unit.

munitions Military equipment, in particular arms and ammunition.

pact A formal agreement between two countries, people, or groups, especially to help each other or to stop fighting.

partisan A member of a body of detached light troops making forays and harassing an enemy.

radar A device that sends out radio waves for finding out the position and speed of a moving object (such as an airplane).

sanctions Actions that are taken to force a country to obey international laws by limiting or stopping trade with that country, by not allowing economic aid for that country, and so forth.

tactics The science and art of disposing and maneuvering forces in combat.

theater The entire land, sea, and air area that is or may become involved directly in war operations.

totalitarianism The political concept that the citizen should be totally subject to an absolute state authority.

war crimes Acts committed during a war that violate international law, usually because they are cruel or unfair.

FOR MORE INFORMATION

Canadian War Museum

1 Vimy Place

Ottawa, ON K1A 0M8

Canada

(800) 555-5621

Website: http://www.warmuseum.ca/home

This museum tells the story of Canada's military history. Along with exhibitions on-site, it has traveling and online exhibitions.

Harry S. Truman Library and Museum

500 W. US Highway 24

Independence, MO 64050

(816) 268-8200

Website: http://www.trumanlibrary.org

This presidential library and museum, in Truman's hometown, has a wealth of information about Harry S. Truman and the events that took place during his presidency, including the final year of World War II.

The Military Museums

4520 Crowchild Trail SW

Calgary, AB T2T 5J4

Canada

(403) 410-2340

Website: http://www.themilitarymuseums.ca

The Military Museums is a Canadian institution that unites eight different museums under one roof. The wars covered span from the Northwest Rebellion of 1885 to the Afghanistan War of the early 2000s.

National Museum of the Pacific War

340 E. Main Street

Fredericksburg, TX 78624

(830) 997-8600

Website: http://www.pacificwarmuseum.org

This museum has been backed by the Admiral Nimitz Foundation since it was established in 1971. Along with Admiral Chester W. Nimitz, the museum also celebrates all of the other men and women who served in the Pacific theater of the war.

The National WWII Museum

945 Magazine Street

New Orleans, LA 70130

(504) 528-1944

Website: http://www.nationalww2museum.org/index.html

FOR MORE INFORMATION | 105

This museum was founded by the historian Stephen Ambrose as The National D-Day Museum in 2000. It has a variety of exhibits and a theater that shows movies about the war.

Special Media Archives Services Division
National Archives at College Park
8601 Adelphi Road
College Park, MD 20740
(301) 837-0561
Website: http://www.archives.gov/research/military/ww2/photos/#aid

World War II is among the best-documented wars in history, in part because of all of the photojournalists who preserved indelible images of the war. The U.S. National Archives' Still Picture unit has tens of thousands of images of World War II, many of which can be accessed online.

WWII History
Sovereign Media
6731 Whittier Avenue, Suite A-100
McLean, VA 22101
Website: http://warfarehistorynetwork.com/magazine/wwii-history-magazine

This magazine, published six times a year, features substantive articles on military history. Its firsthand accounts of incidents in the war, archival photos, and battle maps also help readers get a better understanding of the war.

World War II Veterans Committee

1100 N. Glebe Road, Suite 910

Arlington, VA 22201

(703) 302-1012

Website: http://www.americanveteranscenter.org/wwii-veterans

This project of the American Veterans Center started as the *World War II Chronicles* radio series. It is committed to helping the veterans of World War II tell their stories.

WEBSITES

Because of the changing nature of Internet links, Rosen Publishing has developed an online list of websites related to the subject of this book. This site is updated regularly. Please use this link to access the list:

http://www.rosenlinks.com/WAR/WWII

BIBLIOGRAPHY

Atkinson, Rick. *D-Day: The Invasion of Normandy, 1944*. New York, NY: Henry Holt and Company, 2014.

Atwood, Kathryn J. *Women Heroes of World War II: 26 Stories of Espionage, Sabotage, Resistance, and Rescue* (Women of Action). Chicago, IL: Chicago Review Press, 2011.

Benoit, Peter. *Big Battles of World War II* (True Books). New York, NY: Children's Press, 2014.

Callery, Sean. *World War II* (Scholastic Discover More). New York, NY: Scholastic, 2013.

Hamilton, John. *World War II: Leaders and Generals*. Edina, MN: ABDO, 2011.

Holmes, Richard, et al. *World War II: The Definitive Visual History*. New York, NY: DK Publishing, 2009.

Huey, Lois Miner. *Voices of World War II: Stories from the Front Lines* (Voices of War). Mankato, MN: Capstone Press, 2011.

Makos, Adam, and Marcus Brotherton. *Voices of the Pacific: Untold Stories from the Marine Heroes of World War II*. New York, NY: Berkley Caliber, 2013.

Marrin, Albert. *FDR and the American Crisis*. New York, NY: Knopf, 2014.

Stein, R. Conrad. *World War II* (Cornerstones of Freedom). New York, NY: Scholastic, 2012.

Zamosky, Linda, and Wendy Conklin. *World War II* (Primary Source Readers). Huntington Beach, CA: Teacher Created Materials, 2008.

INDEX

A

Albania, 84
Aleutians, 31, 36
Alexander, Harold, 42
Algeria, 34
Algerian War of Independence, 78
Allies, 6, 11, 12, 24, 29, 34, 36, 37, 38, 40, 41, 43, 44, 48, 54, 64, 84
American Civil War, 49
appeasement, 9
Atlantic, 22, 29, 38, 58, 76
  Battle of the, 29, 37–38
Atlantic Charter, 14, 68
atomic bomb, 48, 57
Australia, 31, 32, 36, 51
Austria, 9, 62, 89, 92
Axis, 6, 18, 20, 25, 26, 32, 33, 36, 37, 84

B

Bataan, 31, 51
battleships, 24, 28, 48
Belgium, 12, 62, 65, 76, 91
Blitz, the, 16
blitzkrieg, 10, 95
Bradley, Omar Nelson, 65
Bulgaria, 20, 41
Bulge, Battle of the, 44
Burma (Myanmar), 31, 40, 45

C

Chamberlain, Neville, 9, 12, 68
Chiang Kai-shek, 18, 41, 72, 74
China, 6, 8, 9, 18, 26, 40, 41, 46, 72, 74
Churchill, Winston, 12, 24, 42, 45, 54, 66, 68–69, 71, 76, 99
Cold War, 8
communism, 57–58, 68, 69, 71
Corregidor, 31
Crete, 25
Czechoslovakia, 9, 62, 65

D

Daladier, Édouard, 9
Danzig, 10
D-Day, 42
de Gaulle, Charles, 14, 76, 78
Denmark, 12, 45, 91
Dunkirk, 12
Dutch East Indies, 31

E

Eastern Front, 34, 42
Egypt, 25, 32–33, 93
Eisenhower, Dwight D., 34, 36, 42, 62, 64–65
El Alamein, 32–33, 93
Eritrea, 84
Ethiopia, 9, 84

F

fascism, 82
Finland, 11, 24, 41, 71, 80
France, 6, 9, 10, 38, 55, 76, 78
   Allied invasion of, 42, 62, 64, 65, 75–76
   battle/fall of, 14, 19, 76, 91
   Nazi occupation of, 16, 18, 34, 44
   World War I in, 55, 60
Free French, 14, 76, 78
French Indochina, 18

G

Germany, 6, 24, 38, 41, 42, 44, 62, 68, 71, 84, 89, 92, 93, 95
   Allied invasion of, 45, 46, 60, 62, 64, 65, 80
   conquest/invasion of other nations, 9–12, 18, 20, 24–25, 76, 91
   and Italy, 10, 18, 19, 86, 88
Gestapo, 95
Gilbert Islands, 36, 58
Göring, Hermann, 16, 93, 95
Great Britain, 6, 11, 12, 24, 25, 42, 68, 71, 81
   Battle of, 14, 16, 95
   and France, 9, 10, 14
   and the United States, 19, 22, 28
Great Depression, 54, 89
Greece, 20, 25
Greenland, 24
Guam, 29, 41

H

Halsey, W.F. (Bull), 35
Hirohito, 26, 48, 96, 98
Hiroshima, 48, 57
Hitler, Adolf, 9, 10, 14, 16, 45, 76, 84, 89, 91–92, 93, 95, 99
Holocaust, 91
Hong Kong, 29
Hull, Cordell, 26
Hungary, 20, 24

I

Iceland, 24
India, 32, 40, 81
Italy, 6, 9, 14, 20, 24, 38, 82, 83, 84
　Allied invasion of, 36–37, 42, 64
　and Germany, 10, 18, 19, 45, 86, 88
Iwo Jima, 46, 58

J

Japan, 6, 24, 41, 58, 84, 86, 88, 96
　and China, 9, 18, 72, 74
　conquest/invasion of other nations, 18, 29, 31, 51
　defeat of, 45, 46, 48, 51, 57, 96
　and the United States, 19, 25–26
Jews, 89, 91
Jodl, Alfred, 45

K

Keitel, Wilhelm, 45
Kesselring, Albert, 36
Korean War, 51, 58

L

League of Nations, 9, 84
Lend-Lease Act, 22
Lenin, Vladimir, 69, 71, 72
Libya, 20, 25, 83
Luftwaffe, 10, 16, 95
Luxembourg, 12, 62, 65

M

MacArthur, Douglas, 35, 36, 41, 46, 49, 51
Manchuria, 18, 48, 72, 86
Marianas, 41, 58
Marshall Islands, 41, 58
Marshall Plan, 57
Mediterranean, 19–20, 32, 34, 36, 75, 95
Midway, 31, 58, 86
Missouri, USS, 48, 58
Montgomery, Bernard, 32, 45, 75–76, 93
Mountbatten, Louis, 81
Mussolini, Benito, 9, 20, 36, 37, 45, 82–84

N

Nagasaki, 48, 57
Nazis, 9, 11, 24, 25, 34, 44, 62, 64, 68, 71, 89, 91, 92, 93, 95

INDEX

Netherlands, 12, 18, 44, 45, 65, 76, 91
New Britain, 31
New Guinea, 31, 32, 35
Nimitz, Chester W., 41, 46, 48, 60
nonaggression pact, 10, 24, 71
Normandy, invasion of, 42–44, 64
Norway, 12, 91

O

Okinawa, 46, 58

P

Pacific, 19, 26, 29, 31, 34–36, 46, 51, 58, 86, 88
Palaus, 58
Patton, George, 60, 62
Pearl Harbor, 26, 28, 29, 51, 54, 58, 86, 88
People's Republic of China, 74
Pétain, Philippe, 14, 76
Philippines, 31, 41, 46, 49, 51, 58, 62
"phony war," 10–11
planes, 14, 16, 19, 22, 28, 31, 38, 40, 41, 46, 57, 86, 95
Poland, 9, 10, 11, 41, 68, 71, 91
Potsdam, 46, 71

R

Red Army, 25, 34, 78, 80
Republic of China, 74
Romania, 20, 24, 41, 71
Rommel, Erwin, 32, 92–93
Roosevelt, Franklin, 22, 24, 26, 42, 51, 52, 54, 55, 57, 68, 71, 99
Royal Air Force (RAF), 16, 38
Russian Revolution, 69, 78
Russo-Japanese War, 84

S

Sandhurst, 66, 75
Sicily, 36, 60, 64, 84
Singapore, 31
Slim, William, 45
Solomon Islands, 35, 36, 58, 86
South African War, 66
Soviet-Finnish War (Winter War), 11, 80
Soviet Union, 6, 8, 11, 34, 41, 48, 71, 80

KEY FIGURES OF WORLD WAR II

German invasion of, 24–25, 71, 91
Spanish-American War, 49
Stalin, Joseph, 10, 42, 45, 54, 68, 69, 71–72, 80
Sudetenland, 9
Sun Yat-sen, 72

T

tanks, 22, 32, 37, 60, 62
Tehran, 42, 71
Tojo Hideki, 25, 86, 88
Tripartite Pact, 18, 86, 88
Trotsky, Leon, 71
Truman, Harry S., 45, 48, 51, 55, 57–58, 71
Truman Doctrine, 57
Tunisia, 64, 65

U

U-boats, 11, 29, 37
United States, 6, 19, 29, 52, 54, 55, 57, 62, 64, 69, 84
  and China, 74
  and Great Britain, 19, 22, 24, 68
  and Japan, 18, 19, 25–26, 28, 48, 57, 86, 96
  and the Soviet Union, 8, 24, 71
  and World War I, 49, 55
United States Military Academy, 49, 60, 62, 65

V

Versailles, Treaty of, 89, 91
Vichy, 14, 34

W

Wake Island, 29
Western Front, 11, 80
World War I, 6, 8, 10, 14, 16, 49, 52, 55, 58, 60, 62, 75, 76, 78, 82, 86, 89, 92, 93

Y

Yalta, 54, 71
Yamamoto Isoroku, 84, 86
Yugoslavia, 20, 42

Z

Zhukov, Georgi Konstantinovich, 78, 80